Taped From Somebody's Brother

Taped From Somebody's Brother

by

Various Artists

First published 2025 by The Hedgehog Poetry Press

Published in the UK by
The Hedgehog Poetry Press
Coppack House, 5
Churchill Avenue
Clevedon
BS21 6QW

www.hedgehogpress.co.uk

9 8 7 6 5 4 3 2 1

A CIP Catalogue record for this book is available from the British Library.

ISBN: 978-1-916830-53-0

Contents

NEIL WINDSOR

Mickey Jupp, Legend.

The least known best known lyricist we got
Hammering out the words on his typewriter drinking blue coffees
In the east wing of his castle for around seventy years and ten
From Red Boot to Oxford to Rockpile Juppanese
Stuck behind a Maserati, searching for Andromeda again

The Guvnor from Sussex then Essex by the sea
Standing at the crossroads again, Elmore James guitar slide
A songwriter and subtle wordsmith of note
Thwarted at every career turn however hard he tried
Unknown as an individual by many, but not the songs he wrote

Revered by Elkie Brooks, Rick Nelson, Edmunds, Feelgood and Lowe
From Down At The Doctors to Switchboard Susan and S.P.Y.
You'll never get him up in one of those things
If God had intended us to fly
He'd have given us the tickets as well as the wings

A touch of Hank Williams, dose of Berry, and boogie woogie walking bass
He doesn't want to do you no harm
Clever word play, subtle phrasing and timing
Just wants to shoot some rock and roll in your arm
From Hallelujah To Amen and West Coast Mainlining

Till Honky Gets Tonky Again.
With the sound of teardrops hitting the floor, late last night
I'd love to boogie, with Guitar Slim, Sonia and Stephanie
Ring Damn You Ring you lump of black bakelite
Tutford Darnell,God and Johnnie Walker, to name a further three

Mickey who? I hear you say
Yet his work and craft you'll surely know
The staple of so many still and down the years
In Boot in Eskdale's Grumpy Corner, sat in open fire's glow
The best and most magnificent of the Southend peers.

WENDY GOULSTONE

A Satyr mourning a Nymph
or The Death of Procris

Piero di Cosimo
National Gallery London

You would think she was
sleeping
 were it not
for the sorrow
in their eyes

his eyes

and the eyes of the dog

The faun looks at her
in a way
that makes your heart
weep

His hand rests
gently
on her shoulder
as if to protect her
to reassure her
that she is not

alone

See how his fingers
stroke
her forehead
gently
gently
as spots of her blood
stain her neck

while the dog
play forgotten
sits still and silent
head bowed
as if in sympathy

If you search for her story
you will learn
the tragedy of it all
tragedy
 heartache

sorrow

How could he see
to paint these
with his eyes
full of tears?

GP HYDE

Magritte Steps Out *

Come with me! Let's take a stroll
with M'sieu Magritte and we'll take in
all manner of marvellous sights
such as you've never seen before.

René Magritte steps outside his front door
with brolly in hand and bowler hat on head.
'Bonjour,' he murmurs as we pass a giraffe in the street.
We glance up. A hundred bowler-hatted men
in long dark coats descend from the clouds.

A racehorse thunders through the streets,
sparks flying from its hooves. The jockey calls out:
Where am I? I'm lost! Where am I going?
The horse strains at the bit, foam flying from its lips.
It's in mid-gallop but moves not a centimetre either way.
Frozen in flight, it hovers over the cobblestones.

Magritte smiles, shrugs his shoulders and walks on.
Another *bourgeois gentilhomme* approaches,
like him, bowler-hatted and in a long dark coat.
A large apple hovers in front of his face. He remains unseen.

We three stroll on and soon arrive by the sandy shore.
'So bracing,' he declares, breathing in the fresh sea air.
A man seated on a rock, cloaked, straw-hatted,
with a birdcage as a ribcage makes no reply.
We gaze out at sea, see a tuba and a kitchen chair,
as high as the Eiffel Tower, hanging above the horizon.

Back home, he puts his key in the lock.
A neighbour with the head and neck of a horse stops to chat.
'Bonjour, monsieur. Back from your walk?
And what are you doing today?'
Magritte smiles and tips his bowler hat to her.
'Life forces me to do something, madame. And so I paint.'

And with that, he enters his house and is gone
to squeeze out paints and squeeze out a vision
from a world so plain and ordinary but holding such magic and mystery.
Let's leave him now, return to our world, replete with his vision.

René Magritte (1898 – 1967) was a Belgian surrealist artist known for his depictions of familiar objects in unfamiliar, unexpected contexts.

TRACI HUGELMAIER

Fade Into You: Hope Sandoval

Packed-in to the quaint, timeless,
The Wiltern standing-theater,
a collective effervescence fills the air,
and meets their holding hands;
it was *their* night to blissfully bare.

Years of his weekly-ritual, ticket-tracking
for this one show, rare,
like their bond...
to hear Mazzy Star play their song:
Fade
    Into
        You

        A song about finding profound love,
        built on not-so-blind faith,
        and a messy, written-on-slate,
        accepting risk of dire heartbreak,
        for the promise of it all,
        of an intense, non-fleeting feeling,
        and a lasting, lifelong love.

        The music, without a single word,
        wholly enchants a crowd of listening hearts;
        the melody graces.
        The tambourine-beats hold the simple rhythm,
        for transfixed faces.
        Then, when the lyrics whisper the simple rhymes,
        they mystically unwind.

If love could be a voice, it might be hers.
Hope.
Preferring near darkness to vanity.
Enchanting, haunting,
Alluring yet demure.
She effortlessly sings the beautiful words like the words don't matter
          and she is the song itself.

Three loves: theirs, the song, and the singer.

GIFFORD SAVAGE

Melanie - No More Candles in the Rain

'*Some came to sing, some came to pray*
Some came to keep the dark away'*
Melanie came to do all three.

When the news came that she was gone –
almost unnoticed and forgotten
because she didn't die young,
the needle coaxed out
warm tones of 54 year old vinyl
while the years spun away.

I was too young for Woodstock,
yet all roads led to Yasgar's Farm,
where Melanie caught the zeitgeist
to sweep me up in visions
of little flames flickering in the rain.
Then I was a beautiful people too.

The record spins and turns,
winding back the years.
The lyrics of my youth recalled –
dancing like sugarplums in my mind,
summoning sanctified memories,
evoking a smile   and a tear.

Ah sweet Melanie! Alone in the dark
I try hard to make the time rhyme,
just like you said you tried to do.
As the stylus pursues the groove
I pour myself a glass of leftover wine,
light a candle to push back the night.

What else is there to do –
when your final show really is done,
and the people have all gone home?

* *from 'Lay Down (Candles in the Rain)' by Melanie Safka*

14

CARMELLA DE KEYSER

House By the Railroad

The oil painting 'House by the Railroad' by Edward Hopper, 1925 is said to have provided the artistic vision for the Bates home in Alfred Hitchcock's 1960 horror film 'Psycho'.

The roof though erect, is sombre, it holds no light,
Yet raindrops christen it,
Their splashes upraise its darkened hues of mossy green and pain.
The sliding windows beat and bruise a bucket of blue,
And rectangular shadows print patterns onto a creaking porch.
Sharp shoulders drooping downwards,
They cannot contain all the regrets this house hides,
For on the bare blood floor Norman Bates was born...
'What character!', and 'such historic features!' passers-by glibly say,
Their compliments fall hollow as coins thrown into a well,
For this house faces north,
Eternally-
It's memories dwell in hell.

MIRIAM MOORE

Home Taping

Before camera phones and polaroids
And selfie sticks and cam corders
My mother bought a tape recorder
And a single C30 tape cassette

We'd sing into the tiny microphone
Her and I. She had an extensive repertoire
Of folk songs and ditties – some obscure -
And unlike me she had perfect pitch

'I will listen to this tape when I'm an old woman' she'd say

But it was me who discovered the tape - It spat and hissed with dust and static
And I had a sudden sickening panic – what if it snapped, or got stuck and tore?
The magnetic tape reveals its secrets. Not my Mother or me
But my Father's surprisingly rich baritone in deepest Geordie
And through the speakers emanates his rendition of 'Adam Buckham-O'

*'Nancy carries watta/Tommy cobbles shoos/But Adam just gans aboot/gathrin' in
the news/O Adam Buckham O / O Adam Buckham O/ O Adam Buckham O/
Wi' his bow legs!*

Then three year old me, in my long lost dialect, interjects
'Them are his old songs'
My Mother will have winced at my grammar. She comments:
'A Northumbrian rendition'
Then he, always needing the last word, objects:
'That's a Tyneside song'.
And I'm sucked into a vortex, a time slip, back to a seventies sitting room
A nuclear family who were far from perfect
She died too young to reminisce
I destroyed the tape. Too much for me to miss.

PHIL SANTUS

The stars, they care

A comment on 'The More Loving One' by W. H. Auden, with reference to 'The Tyger' by William Blake.

Auden, you say that the stars do not care,
yet they are the factories of life.

Their lives are long, and their deaths heroic,
seeding worlds with cosmic hope.

To rephrase the words of Blake, they are the furnace
in which the elements are forged, that is:

Carbon, oxygen and all the rest.

Our universe is astounding and vanishingly improbable,
yet here we are, and nurtured.

What process defined the cosmic laws and
selected from the constants?

When living forms look out and see, they find
our friends, the stars, just right for you and me.

How else could we come to be?

Science, beautiful science,
illuminating the mysteries,
one after another,
and so on, and on....

SHARRON GREEN

Always Take The Weather With You

for Disy, who took me in

A fter closing time and Ahmed's
L ate on a Saturday night
W e'd all stumble back to Southfields
A nd carry on drinking
Y our playlist
S till sings in my head

T ucked around the table
A s our curries settled
K itchen fogged with cigarettes
E mpty cans would

T ower, whisky worked the room
H eads close in banter
E veryone with a story

W ise words and travel tales
E mpty boasts and cutting jokes
A rguments about the haka
T rivia questions turned to Never
H ave I ever... Spin the bottle
E nveloped in music by
R EM, Van Morrison, Crowded House

W *eather with you* was my favourite
I t made me smile then, and now
T akes me back to my twenties
H edonistic, happy days

Y ou're in the Ozzie sun now
O ld age looms rudely
U ntil they play our song

HEATHER MOULSON

Sooty

Thanks to you, Sooty, it was a wonderful 1985.
Especially when I taped that episode
of you crying because you were so small.
Your underrated acting skills second to none.
Soo the Panda got on my nerves.
I rewound that TDK tape so many times

Thank you, Sooty for a marvellous 1987
where you were supposed to be on a diet.
Yet you devilishly dived into that biscuit tin.
Such a masterpiece despite the dropouts.
Sweep the Dog got on my nerves.
I rewound that TDK tape so many times

Sooty, you presented me with a golden 1998.
You had an allure on tape not recaptured
on your YouTube channel (hovering in sight).
Being sick over Matthew Corbett's shoes!
Priceless! Cousin Scampi got on my nerves.
I rewound that TDK tape so many times

PAUL INGS

Zrní, Hýkal

Since when was the fairy tale ever
the horrible thing in itself?
Surely you too once entered the forest
at just that very point of a late
autumnal afternoon
when a few steps take you from day into night
or worse, you entered before this
only to be duped so slowly
and unnoticeably into nightmare
as an enclosed world with no toothy grin
of pale light just behind you
at the edge of the trees to return to;
but even then, if you do get out

the day has already tipped,
and though just an hour ago
the sudden leap of a dog
up, out and over the oats
was a launch into pure joy,
now the crack of the dry plants
and the loose flying flapping tongue
make you start

                    so you call the dog
closer to heel where he stands
quaffing at the air of life
while expulsing lungfuls of steam
into moonlight all ears and eyes
and you realize
it is moonlight you now see by
so you both stand stock still
for there is that thing
that round these parts goes by the name
of Hýkal; and you may perhaps do well
to lend an ear to songs born from those
who have felt its hot breath on their necks
while foraging hungry in dim evening light
not so many moons ago
just beyond the fairytale
in this very world.

OLIVIA TODD

Do You Know?

Do you know what it's like for your core
to be taken on a Viennese waltz?
Do you know what it's like for nostalgia
to cover you like a duvet?
Do you know what it's like when rhythms play
your ribcage like a xylophone?
Do you know what it's like when lyrics send
messages of support to your brain?
Everything will be okay.
Do you know you're a golden underdog?
Do you know you're wanted and loved?
Do you know you're a miracle?
If not, listen to Owl City and P!nk
for they provide an inner link.

TINA MACNAUGHTON

The Story of the Blues
by Pete Wylie and the Mighty WAH!

I sat in my bedroom
at just eighteen years
revising for A levels
with hopes, dreams and fears

Then you came on the radio
with vowels northern and flat
and played all kinds of bands
bit of this, bit of that

You had your little favourites
often obscure, some quite dark
had a high standard of music
and you could be off the mark...

Every so often you played Pete
with his Story of the Blues
the Mighty WAH! filled my room
got me tapping my shoes

Mr Peel, you were a legend
and yes, you loved Pete
The Story of the Blues
or an Eighties' indie masterpiece... ?

MICK YATES

old times

how well i remember those nights

nights of beautiful food, intelligent conversation and bonhomie

the stories flowing as freely as the red wine

our personal origins and histories explored together

the shared experiences of theatre, of dance, of poetry and music

and the sweet mysterious charms of egypt

our communal love of all things conceived in beauty

those subtle subliminal links between humans

drawn and mutually attracted to each other

by their interests, their backgrounds

and their natural curiosity about life

ah those nights how well i remember them

and the great pleasure they brought me

will be held in my heart and mind

for as long as i remain in this world

JULIE ANNE GILLIGAN

Captain Beefheart and His Magic Band

Who? What band? I didn't know
Why would I? How would I?
My vinyl was Soul, Otis, Marvin,
Sam and Dave, Motown, Four Tops.
Supremes. We sang and danced
them all the way home from school.
I knew about the Blues, Mayall,
Butterfield, then Eric the God,
Delaney and Bonnie, George Harrison
at Fairfield Halls with the boy
whose name I forget who said
I must listen to this Magic Band
(and I knew all the words
to the entire Monkees repertoire)
hey hey but this was something else
Don van Vliet squeaks exotica
Trout Mask Replica, why? Erotica?
Moonlight on Vermont squeeeak
psychedelic Corpse, why not?
Album cover weird, by Schenkel:
designer for producer Zappa squeak
Weirder and weirder psychedelia
June 1969 16 and impressionable
for weird men with mad eyes, beards
seductive rhythms, magic smiles
but naïve, too young to understand
the words so all I knew squeak
was the name, the title, until ...
I met my own mad eyed, bearded man
With a magic smile who played
Trout Mask Replica for me. Together,
together still. What more can I say?
What could I say? Even if I wanted to ...

AMANDA HILL

Kabylian Love Song

Such beauty flowing through the air
Your heart so moved by her face, her hair
Your song of love just went unheard
I wish she could have understood
Your passion.
Unrequited love flowed through your hands,
Plucked at the strings of your mystical guitar.
I wept for you.

She never knew your love.
Aged twenty one you bled inside,
Your feelings couldn't be denied
Algerian backdrop, family ties
She'll never know how much you tried
To win her heart.

I played your song to friends back home.
No one seemed as moved as me,
No words, just sounds, a frequency.
I felt your pain.

That twinge again
Years later came,
When on the stage a poet breathed the words
'My angel'.
Another soul lost out in space
That woman too did not take heed.

I longed for love as deep as that
A song, some words, devotion brushed with silver-coated magic dust
The future filled with warmth and trust
Eternal love
Secure, serene.
Blissful moments never seen
When young, naive, unfettered hearts
Are pierced by the poison darts
Shot from the eyes of deaf young girls
Who could not hear their pain.

Those poignant notes,
The haunting sound of your guitar
Invades my dreams,
Uplifts my soul, or so it seems
As I drift off once more.

MANDY WILLIS

Tea for the Tillerman

Album by Cat Stevens, later Yusuf.

I make tea I'd never drink for my Tillerman.
Eleven gentle reflective hues
Released like me at the cusp of the contradictory seventies.
Unconscious compass of folk-like complexity.

As I left my happy home to see what I could find
It cautioned me to the wild world and possible envywhere.
It suggested taking time, and being more than just a smile.
Advised looking for connections rather than just reaching there.

It chimed that hard work is not just doing what they say.
Raised my eyes to mountaintops and questions of why.
The seductive glint of friendliness that could easily distract
From the search to become my own hard headed woman.

When my eyes were windows trickling grey rain.
It let free my unique sorrow no one else could claim.
As I felt miles from nowhere lost in foggy white.
It gave time to slowly build a house with windows gleaming light.

Now they leave our happy home as timorously I wait.
It warns against ordering them to listen.
Preaching limits as they create space to play.
Mother dreams conjuring acres of sky with much left to know.

Aged fifty reshaped through unprecedented times,
I found the power of turning fear into the sublime.
Nostalgically now I listen end to end.
Find hardwired voices from now, there and then.

'Seagulls sing my heart away.
I found my head when I wasn't trying'.

KATE COPELAND

Can I call you Superlungs?

A poem to the album "Seed of Memory"

Turning down Deep Purple, Zeppelin, yet
opening for Stones in States — all urban
myths aside, his mum just did not like him
to go world at such young age. He accepted
tours' ways, wrote his own way.

A 60s-70s rock-soul boy, Aretha adored him
- white man with soul - he makes you believe
every single, a music moving forward, magic
guitars and lungs, a get-what-you-see sound.

No opportunity to turn into Stones-status,
solo albums turned into escape instead of
release. Yet, Terry Reid calls own shots, he
perfections rhythm-cord structures, songs
in his heart, never go away.